Little Pebble™

Little Critters

Earthworms

by Lisa J. Amstutz

CAPSTONE PRESS
a capstone imprint

Little Pebble is published by Capstone Press,
1710 Roe Crest Drive, North Mankato, Minnesota 56003
www.mycapstone.com

Library of Congress Cataloging-in-Publication Data
Names: Amstutz, Lisa J., author.
Title: Earthworms / by Amstutz, Lisa.
Description: North Mankato, Minnesota : Capstone Press, [2017] | Series:
  Little pebble. Little critters | Audience: Ages 4-8.? | Audience: K to
  grade 3.? | Includes bibliographical references and index.
Identifiers: LCCN 2016001320| ISBN 9781515719380 (library binding) | ISBN
  9781515719427 (pbk.) | ISBN 9781515719465 (ebook pdf)
Subjects: LCSH: Earthworms—Juvenile literature.
Classification: LCC QL391.A6 A47 2017 | DDC 592/.64—dc23
LC record available at http://lccn.loc.gov/2016001320

Editorial Credits
Carrie Braulick Sheely, editor; Juliette Peters, designer;
Wanda Winch, media researcher; Tori Abraham, production specialist

Photo Credits
© Dwight Kuhn, 5, 10, 15, 19, 21; Alamy: Nature Photographers, Ltd, 17; Minden Pictures: Ch'ien Lee, 13; Newscom: H/blickwinkel/picture alliance/H. Schmidbauer, 9; Shutterstock: blackeagleEMJ, 1, clearviewstock, 11, kzww, back cover (worm), 3 (all), 22, Number1411, soil image used as background throughout book, Picsfive, note design, schankz, 7, wawritto, cover

Printed in China.
007690

Table of Contents

Dig It!

Dig! Dig! Earthworms make holes in soil. The holes make good homes.

Worms like wet dirt.

Hot sun dries their skin.

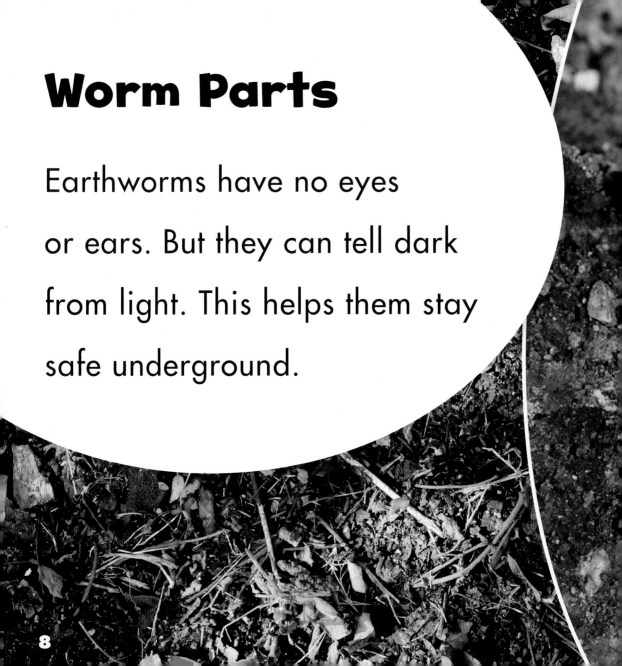

Worm Parts

Earthworms have no eyes or ears. But they can tell dark from light. This helps them stay safe underground.

Wiggle! Tiny hairs help worms move.

They grip the soil.

hair

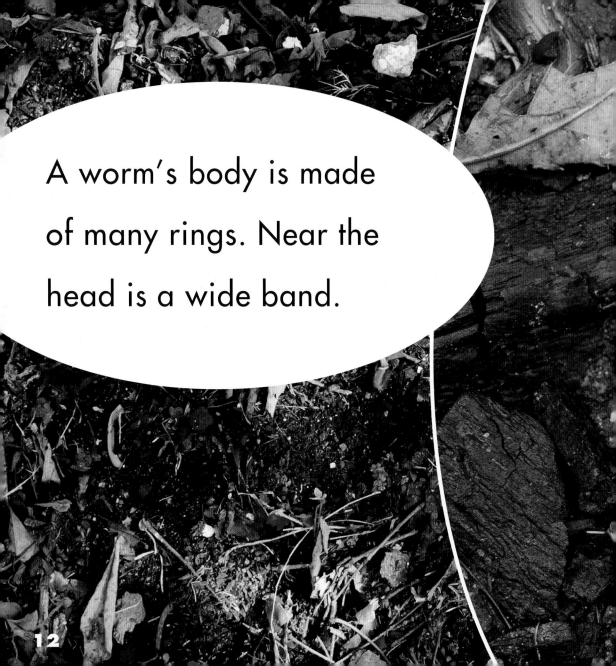

A worm's body is made of many rings. Near the head is a wide band.

13

Lunch Time

Munch! Earthworms eat dead plants.

They eat tiny rocks too.

The rocks grind the food.

Worms eat and eat.

Their poop helps plants grow.

worm

Baby Worms

Earthworms lay eggs.

The eggs are in a cocoon.

19

Baby worms hatch out.

They eat, dig, and grow.

Glossary

band—a thick ring

cocoon—a covering made of slime; worms make a cocoon to hold their eggs until they are ready to hatch

grind—to crush or wear down

hatch—to come out of an egg

soil—another word for dirt

Read More

Goldish, Meish. *Inside the Worm's Hole.* Snug as a Bug: Where Bugs Live. New York: Bearport Publishing, 2014.

McCloskey, Kevin. *We Dig Worms!* New York: RAW Junior, LLC, 2015.

Smith, Sian. *Worms.* Creepy Critters. Chicago: Raintree, 2013.

Internet Sites

FactHound offers a safe, fun way to find Internet sites related to this book. All of the sites on FactHound have been researched by our staff.

Here's all you do:
Visit *www.facthound.com*
Type in this code: 9781515719380

Check out projects, games and lots more at
www.capstonekids.com

Critical Thinking
Using the Common Core

1. How do worms help plants grow? (Key Ideas and Details)

2. How do rocks help worms eat? (Key Ideas and Details)

Index